The Christmas Story

REFLECTIONS FOR ADVENT

KEITH McILROY
& ANDREW DICKSON

AMBASSADOR INTERNATIONAL
GREENVILLE, SOUTH CAROLINA & BELFAST, NORTHERN IRELAND

www.ambassador-international.com

The Christmas Story

Reflections for Advent

Paperback: ISBN: 978-1-64960-193-3

Printed in UK

Ambassador International
Emerald House
411 University Ridge, Suite B14
Greenville, SC 29601
www.ambassador-international.com

Ambassador Books and Media
The Mount
2 Woodstock Link
Belfast, BT6 8DD, Northern Ireland, UK
www.ambassadormedia.co.uk

Dedicated to the congregation of
High Kirk Presbyterian Church, Ballymena,
Northern Ireland, who first encouraged us.

Soli Deo Gloria

Contents

Part 1 Back to the Beginning

1st Dec Glory revealed (John 17:5)
2nd Dec Life without Christmas (Genesis 1:31)
3rd Dec War is over, if you want it (Genesis 3:15)
4th Dec From bad to worse (Genesis 6:5)
5th Dec Blessing the world (Genesis 22:18)

Part 2 Christmas Foretold

6th Dec An everlasting kingdom (2 Samuel 7:12-13)
7th Dec God with us (Isaiah 7:14)
8th Dec Light for the world (Isaiah 9:2)
9th Dec Humble beginnings (Isaiah 11:1)
10th Dec The Shepherd King (Micah 5:2, 4a)

Part 3 Preparing for Christmas

11th Dec Preparing the way (Luke 1:17)
12th Dec An adoptive dad (Matthew 1:20)
13th Dec Leaping for joy (Luke 1:44)
14th Dec A mother's song (Luke 1:53)
15th Dec Two kinds of peace (Luke 2:1)

Part 4 Christmas Come

16th Dec The word became flesh (John 1:14)

17th Dec Making God known (John 1:18)

18th Dec Peace on earth, peace in heaven (Luke 2:14)

19th Dec The original Scrooge (Matthew 2:3)

20th Dec Christmas worship (Matthew 2:11)

Part 5 The Message of Christmas

21st Dec Telling the story (Luke 2:17-18)

22nd Dec Ponder these things (Luke 2:19)

23rd Dec From the cradle to the cross (John 19:26-27)

24th Dec The purpose of the story (Luke 24:25-27)

25th Dec The Second Advent (Colossians 3:4)

Christmas
[feast of Christ]

Hurry, Star, for we wait below,
The earth in sin is pining
For light to rise upon her face
And crown the dawn of Promise.

The Law and Prophets written,
Words set, the tablets marked,
Jew, Gentile, Roman; all ready
For that coming day to start.

The babe with power, in frailty set,
Adam once again has come
To die, but know this one will us redeem-
Where Adam failed, the babe shall win.

Prepare to see Emmanuel.
Pause. For God is with us. Some day
To eat his flesh and drink his blood,
To usher in the feast of Christ.

Hurry, Star, we wait below,
The earth in sin is pining.

Introduction

"We've lost the real meaning of Christmas." I'm sure you hear words similar to these almost every year and you might even have said them yourself on more than one occasion. It can be so easy to get distracted at Christmas time with all the present buying, food preparation, and organising family gatherings (or not, as the case may be). In the midst of all the noise, colour, and festive cheer it can be hard to focus our minds and hearts on the true meaning of Christmas, the reason we have such a season called 'Christmas' in the first place. Christian communities that follow the church calendar have more success in focusing the attention of the people on the meaning of Christmas because they make a big deal of 'Advent', the season of anticipation and preparation for the coming of Christ.

This short set of 25 reflections will cover much of this period that is designated 'Advent' and give the reader a biblical nugget to chew on each day on the run in to Christmas. Many of the verses reflected on here might be very familiar to some readers. One unique feature of these reflections is that they will broadly follow the flow of Scripture and tell the Christmas story from beginning to end. There will also be a poem at the end of each reflection which will give the reader a different perspective on the meaning of each passage.

It can be difficult sometimes to stop and think about the most important things at Christmas time, so if all that the reader gains from these short thoughts is an opportunity to pause in the busyness of each day to raise their eyes toward the King of Kings, it will be worth it. So let's begin at the beginning…

Part 1

Back to the Beginning

GLORY REVEALED

1st December

Read: John 17

'And now, Father, glorify me in your presence with the glory I had with you before the world began.'

John 17:5

When I was growing up, if you wanted to watch a movie at home you either had to wait for it to come out on terrestrial TV (on one of four channels) – which would usually mean waiting several years – or buy it on VHS. Now you can stream movies almost instantaneously. However, between the VHS and streaming there was the magical 'DVD'. The one advantage of this format is the fact that most DVD's come with 'extras'. If you're a big movie fan like me, then you'll love the special features that come with your favourite films. They offer an insight into the making of the film as the director will often provide a commentary to accompany the film and a 'making of" featurette. You can gain new insights which, from my perspective, often enhance the pleasure of watching the story with fresh understanding.

In many ways, Jesus' prayer in John 17 is like the director's commentary when it comes to thinking about the Bible's big story, and the Christmas story more specifically. Here Jesus is in conversation with his Father and is praying for his immediate disciples and those who will come to believe the message they will proclaim (17:20). In this incredible chapter Jesus pulls back the curtain of eternity to give us a glimpse of the life of the Triune God before the world was even created. Jesus says to the Father that he has brought him glory on earth by completing the work he had been given to do and then comments, 'And now, Father, glorify me in your presence with *the glory I had with you before the creation of the world*' (v. 5). The Son enjoyed glory with the Father (and the Spirit) before the world was created. If you ever wondered what God was doing before he created us and the universe, he was enjoying his own infinite glory and love. God is perfect in love and glory and therefore he had absolutely no need to create us. Yet he chose to create us out of his own lavish grace so that we could share in enjoying and experiencing his love and glory (v. 24). That is what Christmas is really all about – God revealing his glory to humanity. We too often jump straight into the gospel accounts and miss the backstory that makes sense of all the other wonderful events that occur around the birth of Christ.

As you enter into this advent season, pause and reflect on the fact that the eternal, majestic, and perfect God chose to create us and enter our world in order to reveal to us his glory so that we could participate in his love. Long before a baby was placed in a manger, the infinite God had planned to make known his own greatness to his finite creatures. Now that's a story worth telling!

- I -

Before bright brilliant starburst songs,
The cosmos' vast expanse,
The Father, Son and Spirit; One,
With perfect counsel announce:

A race that will God's creatures be,
Brought forth that they His glory see.

LIFE WITHOUT CHRISTMAS

2nd December

READ: Genesis 1

'God saw all that he had made, and it was very good...'

Genesis 1:31

Can you imagine a life without Christmas? What would it be like and what would you miss the most? I'm sure that for many people they would miss the excitement, the hustle and bustle, the days spent with family, the exchange of presents, the decorated tree or familiar tunes that fill the airways. But I'm not really talking about any of that. Even if Christmas didn't exist, people would still end up of doing many of these things regardless. What I'm really getting at is: can you imagine a world in which Christ had never been born? What would that be like and what would we miss? Ask any number of secular thinkers today and the answer they'd give would likely be, 'Very little'. But is that actually true? Think about it. If Christmas hadn't happened – if Christ hadn't been born – we wouldn't have: the universal education system we have today (especially universities), we wouldn't have modern science and medicine, we wouldn't have the basic concept of 'human rights', workers right and social care. All of these things were driven forward by men and women who believed that the baby born in Bethlehem had come to change the world and they lived in light of this truth. In the end, a life without

Christmas would mean a life without a lot of other things we take for granted. But we're getting ahead of ourselves…

The only two people to have ever experienced a life without Christmas – or more specifically, a life without the need for Christmas – were the first two human beings. Genesis 1 tells the story of the good Creator taking pleasure in all that he made as a means of revealing his glory. At the end of each day of creation we read the same refrain, 'And God saw that it was good.' However, on the last day of creation we read these words, 'God saw all that he had made, and it was *very good* (Genesis 1:31).' What made this final day 'very good'? God had created the pinnacle of his creation – human beings made in his own image (1:27). God made creatures to not only enjoy his glory but to display it as well. There was no need for Christmas because everything was 'very good'. Not yet as good as it could be (Adam still had to fulfil his calling), but very good nonetheless. Unless we understand that Christmas was needed because the very good world soon became a very bad one (Genesis 3) then we'll never understand its true purpose. But again we're getting ahead of ourselves…

Here's a question for you to consider in light of our reflection: What would my life be like without Jesus? What if he had never taken on human flesh and been born in Bethlehem? What would that mean for me culturally, socially, personally and spiritual? These are questions well worth pondering.

- II -

A debt incurred comes with us still,
Our wages cast us down.
Weep who once dwelt in paradise,
Who sought too great a crown.

What hope to hold among the dark?
What light could make us clean, unmarked?

WAR IS OVER, IF YOU WANT IT

3rd December

READ: Genesis 3

'And I will put enmity between you and the woman, and between your offspring and hers; he will crush your head, and you will strike his heel.'

Genesis 3:15

What marks the beginning of Christmas for you? I wish I could say that for me it was something holy and profound but if I'm perfectly honest it's when I hear a certain song on the radio. Christmas began for me today because I turned on the radio and heard the dulcet tones of Michael Bublé sing, 'It's beginning to look a lot like Christmas…' Songs have a powerful way of shaping our experiences and the way we view the world. Christmas songs are no exception. However, if we stopped to think about the lyrics of our favourite songs would we really agree with Wizzard that we wish it could be Christmas *every* day? (I know some people who would want this to be the case). One of the most popular Christmas songs, played every year since its release, is John Lennon's 'Happy Xmas (War is Over)'. Lennon never intended his song to simply fill up a space on the annual 'Ultimate Christmas Songs Ever' album but was trying to communicate a deeper message. Lennon was expressing the desire for peace on earth and he believed (naively) that it could be achieved if we only willed it to be the case. As the constant refrain declares,

'War is over, if you want it.' The problem is, no matter how much we might wish that war would finally end, it just keeps rearing its ugly head.

But why is there war in the first place? If we return to the beginning of the story we find God's good people, living in God's good place, enjoying God's good presence.[1] There was no war, sickness, death or sin. God had given his people everything good to enjoy and called them to be fruitful, increase in number, fill the earth and subdue it (Gen. 1:28). However, he also commanded them not to eat of the tree of the knowledge of good and evil on pain of death (2:16-17). Humanity wanted for nothing but God withheld one thing from them in order to remind them that he was God and that they ought always to submit to his rule as creator and provider. As we know, they chose to listen to the whispers of the serpent (3:1-7) and plunged all their descendants, and the world, into sin and death (3:16-19). There would now be a constant war between the offspring of the woman and the offspring of the serpent (the devil). That could have been the end of the story. But God, being rich in mercy and love, promised that one of the woman's descendants would one day crush the head of their enemy and restore all that was broken (3:15). War would indeed be over, but only through God's promised redeemer. That means that advent began at Genesis 3:15. When does Christmas begin for you? It might be much earlier than you think!

- III -

Silent, creature! And hold the tongue
That weaves the web of lies and death.
A battle song picks up its pace,
Declared in strength by God's own breath:

Above the rage of death and doom,
Hero shall come through Eve's own womb.

FROM BAD TO WORSE

4th December

READ: Genesis 6

'The LORD saw how great the wickedness of the human race had become on the earth, and that every inclination of the thoughts of the human heart was only evil all the time.'

Genesis 6:5

Have you ever had one of those days when you thought nothing could get worse…and then it did? You wake up to discover that you forgot to set your alarm and it's much later than you had hoped. You fling the bedcover aside with haste and as you jump out of bed you stub your toe against the wardrobe letting out a less than Christian phrase. You dress in such a hurry that when you're about to walk out the door you glance in the mirror and see that your top has a whopping great stain in the middle that's too obvious to hide. You run upstairs to change, making you even later, only to discover you don't have anything appropriate to wear and have to resign yourself to the silly Christmas jumper. You run out to the car and discover that you don't have your keys. A lengthy and frustrating search begins until you realise that they were in your pocket the whole time. You try to start the engine but the car is having none of it. The day before the car started without a fuss and tomorrow (when you're on time) it will start with ease, but not today – the day you're running late. After sitting behind annoyingly slow moving vehicles you make it to where you need to go only to discover that the meeting is already over. It's just one of those days when things go from bad to worse.

We left our story in a pretty bad place. Humanity had brought a curse upon the earth and had been banished from the paradise God had created for them (Genesis 3:23). Surely things couldn't get worse. Unfortunately they could. The first son of the woman – whom she thought was going to be God's promised Saviour (4:1) – ends up killing his younger brother out of jealousy, committing the first murder. Humanity goes from bad to worse until we are eventually told, 'The LORD saw how great the wickedness of the human race had become on the earth, and that every inclination of the thoughts of the human heart was only evil all the time…So the LORD said, "I will wipe from the face of the earth the human race I have created…for I regret that I have made them"' (6:5, 7). Again, this could have been the end of the story, but God had made a promise to his people that he was going to send someone to sort out the mess. In his grace, God spared the life of Noah and his descendants and promised them that he would never again destroy the world, even though the wickedness of humanity would continue (8:21). Unlike us, God never breaks his promises and Christmas day is the evidence of his faithfulness and love. Christmas assures us that even when things go from bad to worse God can intervene to bring us to a better place.

- IV -

Blot them out, these loved of mine
Who rage and toil against my face.
Purify and wash them clean,
That remnant left, my chosen race.

They will remain my people still;
My Promise made, I will fulfil.

BLESSING THE WORLD

5th December

READ: Genesis 12

'...and through your offspring all nations on earth will be blessed, because you have obeyed me.'

Genesis 22:18

One of the most exciting things about Christmas is the giving and receiving of gifts. Some people are gifted gift givers. My brother for instance is very good at choosing gifts. He also manages to get his Christmas shopping out of the way long before the rest of us. I, on the other hand, am terrible. If it wasn't for my wife I would most likely forget to buy anyone a gift (including her). It's not that I don't care (though you might dispute that) but that I get occupied with so many other things. Maybe others are just more generous spirited than me, but what I find interesting is; what ought to be a joyous experience can often turn into an obligation. Think about it. When you've finished all your Christmas shopping and you're sure that you've covered everyone you can possibly think of, what do you do when you receive an unexpected gift from someone who wasn't on your list? If you're honest, you don't just receive it gratefully with a smile. You're probably grimacing inside and thinking, 'Ahh, now I have to go out and find them something in return!' Instead of gift giving being an opportunity to bless, it can become a grudging obligation to save face. Even Christians can get so caught up in the annual routine that we forget that we have been blessed by God to be a blessing.

Yesterday we left humanity in a pretty bad state. Things had gone from bad to worse and there seemed to be little sign of God's promised deliverer who was going to set all things right. But that all changes just a few chapters later in Genesis 12 when God calls a man named Abram (later Abraham). God tells this man to leave his family and go to a land that he will give to him and his offspring. In fact, God promises this man the same things he had promised the first humans – innumerable descendants, a special land, and God's own presence (12:1-3; 15:5; 17:6-7, 8; 22:17). But why did God make these promises to Abraham? God was blessing Abraham that he might be a blessing to others (12:3). He was telling Abraham that the promise of Christmas would one day be fulfilled through him. Not directly through Abraham - who would only see a shadow of the promise to come - but through one of his descendants. As God says to him in Genesis 22:18, '…through your offspring all the nations on earth will be blessed…' The apostle Paul makes clear that the 'offspring' referred to here is none other than Jesus Christ (Galatians 3:16). This promise to bless all the nations – which Paul calls the gospel (Galatians 3:8) – could only begin to have its fulfilment on Christmas day. The blessed redeemer would be born to be a blessing, and he calls all who trust in him to be a blessing as well. How might we bless this year?

- V -

Count the stars or grains of sand-
Your lineage that gives you mirth,
One grain, one seed, will fall and die
And rise again to bless the earth.

Abraham, father of the line
That will redeem in God's own time.

Part 2

Christmas Foretold

AN EVERLASTING KINGDOM

6th December

READ: 2 Samuel 7

'When your days are over and you rest with your ancestors, I will raise up your offspring to succeed you, your own flesh and blood, and I will establish his kingdom. He is the one who will build a house for my Name, and I will establish the throne of his kingdom forever.'

2 Samuel 7:12-13

Trees. It seems that in almost every house in the Western world there is a decorated tree at Christmas time. But why? Of course, we know that trees are important in the Bible. We've already thought about the tree of the knowledge of good and evil in Genesis (2:17); Jesus was hung on a tree when he was crucified (Galatians 3:13); and when Christ ushers in the new heaven and earth we will eat from the tree of life (Revelation 22:14). But that's not the reason we have decorated trees at Christmas. The true origins of the Christmas tree are hard to trace but legend has it that the great German Reformer Martin Luther came up with the idea while preparing a sermon in the forest one evening. Struck by seeing the stars shining through the branches he tried to replicate it at home for his family. Yet even this doesn't answer the question why so many people have made the decorated tree an essential part of Christmas. The real reason for its popularity stems from the fact that Queen Victoria was so fond of the practice that when she and her husband Albert were pictured standing beside their lavishly decorated tree, everyone wanted one. Kings and queens can wield a powerful influence over their subjects, even over subsequent generations.

Its several generations before the promises made to Abraham begin to come to fruition. God's people endure famine, slavery, freedom from slavery, and years of wandering in the desert before they finally take possession of the land God promised (Joshua 21:43). However, after a few good years under the leadership of Joshua (Josh. 24:31) things start to go wrong. Under the Judges who followed Joshua things go from bad to worse. It seems like a case of déjà vu. At the end of his book, the author of Judges diagnoses the problem, 'In those days Israel had no king; everyone did what was right in his own eyes.' That wasn't strictly true because God had been Israel's king (1 Samuel 8:7), but it seemed that the people had rejected him. It isn't long before God's people ask for a different king, one like all the other nations around them (1 Sam. 8:5). So God gave them Saul. To say that Saul was a disaster would be an understatement. However, God being ever rich in love and grace, gave Israel another king, this time a man after his own heart – David (1 Sam. 13:14). But even this king would have feet of clay. Nevertheless, God promised David that one of his descendants would come and establish his throne forever (2 Sam. 7:12-13). This would be the king to come at Christmas, someone who would exercise an eternal and universal influence…

- VI -

Lie still beneath the earth in peace,
Lie with your kin and be at rest
Though anxious none have brought the day
Through which the nations will be blessed.

Take heart for seasons still remain;
In time redemption will be plain.

Like sun rays reach at break of day
To chase the shadows from the sky,
The eternal throne will soon appear,
Your flesh and blood soon lifted high.

GOD WITH US

7th December

READ: Isaiah 7

'Therefore the Lord himself will give you a sign: The virgin will conceive and give birth to a son, and will call him Immanuel.'

Isaiah 7:14

'If you want a thing done well, do it yourself.' So said Napoleon Bonaparte; allegedly. There are certain things in life that I'm more than happy for other people to do for me (Christmas shopping would be one of them). However, there are other things that I just wouldn't trust others to do in the way I'd like. The problem with this type of thinking is that, shocking as it might be, my way might not be the best way. And I'm not the only one to suffer from this way of thinking. In the book 'The Narcissism Epidemic' the authors highlight a study of international pupils which showed that American children had the greatest confidence in their own abilities but achieved some of the lowest grades while Korean children had the lowest opinion of their abilities and yet achieved the best results. The authors (who themselves are American) concluded, 'We're not number one, but we're number one in *thinking* we are number one.'[2] In many respects this is a problem that marks the broader culture of our Western world.

As we discovered yesterday, the people of Israel fell into this type of thinking. Remember the stark words of the author of Judges, '...everyone did what was right in his own eyes.' The author diagnosed the problem: '...Israel had no king...' But even when they had a king things didn't really change. God had warned his people about what would happen if the king started to do what was right in his own eyes (Deut. 17:14-20). Unfortunately, even their greatest king, Solomon, committed each of the sins warned about in the law. This resulted in the dividing of Israel's kingdom and set in motion generations of mostly bad kings sitting on the thrones of Judah and Israel. By the time we reach the period of the prophet Isaiah, the northern tribes of Israel have been taken into exile and the southern tribes of Judah are facing a massive threat to their existence. In Isaiah 7 God speaks to King Ahaz through the prophet and calls him to stand firm and trust his word. Instead, Ahaz puts his trust in their sworn enemy Assyria. The king goes his own way. Therefore God makes an incredible promise to the house of David, 'the Lord *himself* will give you a sign: The virgin will conceive and give birth to a son, and will call him Immanuel.' God speaks of a day when a miraculous birth will take place and a child will be born who will be known as 'Immanuel' – 'God with us.' What God was promising his people was that he would come and rescue them from their sins and from themselves (see, Isa. 59:16; 63:5). God had to do this work himself. He had to do for us what we could never do for ourselves. And he would do it through the coming of Jesus (Matt. 1:22-23). This is the glorious hope of Christmas – God with us and for us!

- VII -

No king of man of royal blood,
No sage, no fame, nor skill contain
The power to lift us from the mud,
To loose the earth from sin's fell reign.

What hope? What hope? Where shall we cling?
What fount brings forth a cleansing spring?

The Lord himself will come down then,
The Lord of hosts, God with us through
A virgin, this child no son of men,
Will do the work we could not do.

LIGHT FOR THE WORLD

8th December

READ: Isaiah 9

'The people walking in darkness have seen a great light; on those living in the land of deep darkness a light has dawned.'

Isaiah 9:2

In the opening scene of his 1993 masterpiece, Schindler's List, Steven Spielberg presents us with a Jewish family standing around a lit candle as the head of the household leads in prayer. The camera then focuses in on the candle, particularly the brightly burning wick, which is the only piece of colour left in the frame. As the candle burns down the flame becomes less and less bright until it eventually goes out altogether. This causes a plumage of smoke to drift upwards and the film cuts immediately to a matching plumage of smoke emanating from a steam train pulling into a station where Jewish people are being transported to one of the Nazi's horrific ghettos. These opening few frames are some of the best in film history not only because of the clever visual juxtaposition between images but because of the moral metaphor that lies behind the extinguishing of the candle light. As the physical light goes out so, metaphorically, the light of the Jewish people goes out as they are plunged into one of the darkest periods in human history – the holocaust. Of course, this is not the first time that light, or the lack of it, has been used as a metaphor. It is as old as the Old Testament scriptures.

Yesterday we read God's incredible promise to send a child who would bring his presence among the people (Isa. 7:14). If you have been paying close attention to the Christmas story so far you'll remember that God had already promised a child who would defeat the enemy of his people and restore his broken world (Genesis 3:15). But before this would happen the people were going to have to endure some very dark times. Instead of trusting in God's promise the people went after other gods and dabbled in forbidden spiritual practices (Isa. 8:19-21). God warned the people that this would lead to '…distress and darkness and fearful gloom, and they will be thrust into utter darkness' (8:22). But the people wouldn't listen. This led to the destruction of the temple (the place where God's glory dwelt), exile to Babylon, and oppression under the Persians, Greeks, and eventually the Romans. However, as we have seen throughout this story, God is full of grace and mercy towards his people. Through the prophet Isaiah he spoke again of a time when he would restore his rebellious people, when the people walking in darkness would see a great light (9:2). And as before, that light would come through a promised child. Isaiah declares those famous words we read every Christmas, 'For to us a child is born, to us a son is given, and the government will be on his shoulders. And he will be called Wonderful Counsellor, Mighty God, Everlasting Father, Prince of Peace' (9:6). He would be the serpent crushing, world restoring, light of the world (John 8:12). O, what a Saviour!

- VIII -

The songs that spoke of Promise fall
Upon deaf ears that soon forgot
The God who rescued Israel,
Dark days have been their recent lot.

But wait! What light, what flicker makes
The shadows flee, and us awakes?

The light, though small like babe at breast,
Grows strong and will not be restrained
By aught, until across the earth-
"A light has dawned!" shall be proclaimed.

HUMBLE BEGINNINGS

9th December

READ: Isaiah 11

'A shoot will come up from the stump of Jesse; from his roots a Branch will bear fruit.'

Isaiah 11:1

What are some of the first things that come to mind when you think back to your childhood Christmases? For me, one of the first things is the Chronicles of Narnia by C. S. Lewis. This is somewhat strange because I didn't read the books at Christmas time but I think it's because Father Christmas appears in The Lion, the Witch, and the Wardrobe and the two have forever become connected in my mind. For the generation that came after me it might well be reading the Harry Potter books by J. K. Rowling (or at least watching the films). Unlike Lewis, Rowling did not come from the type of privileged background that most would expect to be typical of a successful children's author. Hers has been described as a 'rags to riches story.' Before writing her bestselling series Rowling was a struggling single mum living on welfare in Edinburgh. The first of the Harry Potter books was rejected by several leading publishers before it was picked up by Bloomsbury. Once it was published it became an immediate success and the rest is history. Rowling may have started from humble beginnings but now she is one of the most widely recognised and respected authors in the world.

Why when the long-promised redeemer of Israel finally arrived on the scene did so few of his people recognise him? Part of the reason might be that most people would have expected Israel's Messiah to be born in a palace, not laid in an animal feeding trough in a cattle shed. In a way you can't blame them for this misunderstanding. Just take the prophecy of the coming child we looked at yesterday in Isaiah 9. After giving him the most lavish of titles ('Wonderful Counsellor…') Isaiah goes on to say, 'Of the greatness of his government and peace there will be no end. He will reign on David's throne and over his kingdom, establishing and upholding it with justice and righteousness from that time on and forever' (Isa. 9:7). However, if they had read a little further in the story they would have realised that this king was not going to be like every other king. After warning God's people that a day was coming when they would be cut down like a tree with nothing but a stump remaining, the prophet declares, 'A shoot will come from the stump of Jesse; from his roots a Branch will bear fruit' (11:1). This single shoot would be anointed by the Spirit with wisdom, counsel, and power (11:2) and he would be the one to judge and transform the world (11:3-9). But he would start humbly and be humbled – 'He grew up before him like a tender shoot, and like a root out of dry ground…He was despised and rejected by men, a man of sorrows, and familiar with suffering' (53:2-3). The Conquering King would first be the Suffering Servant. It would be - cradle to cross to crown.

- IX -

What kingly jewel would fit his brow,
This babe whose life has just begun?
What axe or sword would forge his way,
Whose eyes are yet to see the sun?

Yet in the crib the baby lay,
Full able to keep death at bay.

No legion trained at his command,
No coup d'etat to end their strife,
But live to please the Law's demand
And in his death rise King of Life.

THE SHEPHERD KING

10th December

READ: Micah 5

'But you, Bethlehem Ephrathah, though you are small among the clans of Judah, out of you will come for me one who will be ruler over Israel, whose origins are from of old, from ancient times...He will stand and shepherd his flock in the strength of the LORD...'

Micah 5:2, 4a

Did you have a nickname growing up? Sadly (or thankfully) I never did. The closest thing I got to a nickname for a while was being described as 'Mackie's wee brother.' Nicknames most often make reference to some kind of characteristic in the given person. For instance, I knew someone at school who was always referred to as 'Spud'. Why? Because he looked like a potato. Another friend had the nickname 'Bungle' because he bore a striking resemblance to the bear in the 1980s children's TV show 'Rainbow.' In certain cases the nickname might just be a contraction of their first name or, in some of the less flattering cases, point to something negative in their personality. Throughout the Bible God's people are often referred to as 'sheep'. In one sense this is not a particularly flattering designation. Sheep are not renowned for their intelligence and can often end up wandering off in the wrong direction. An example of this is found in Isaiah 53:6, 'We all, *like sheep*, have gone astray, each of us has turned to his own way...' But in another sense, the term 'sheep' is a title of affection. Earlier in Isaiah the prophet speaks of how God tenderly cares for his people like sheep – 'He tends his flock like a shepherd: He gathers the lambs in his arms and carries them close to his heart; he gently leads those that have young' (Isa. 40:11).

What God's people needed more than anything else was someone to direct them and lead them in the right way. Like sheep, they so often got distracted and wandered off down a dangerous path. In one of the most famous Christmas prophecies, Micah speaks of a day when God will provide his people with the one who will bring them back to him. What is so incredible about this prophecy is its specificity. Micah describes the exact location of the Messiah's birth: 'But you, *Bethlehem* Ephrathah, though you are small among the clans of Judah, out of you will come for me one who will be ruler over Israel...' (Micah 5:2a; see, Matt. 2:6). The fact that he was to be born in Bethlehem, the birthplace of the great king David, wouldn't be all that surprising to his first audience. What was surprising, however, was the description of this coming ruler. Micah goes on, '...whose origins are from of old from ancient days' (5:2b). Amazingly Micah attributes to the Messiah what elsewhere only ever refers to God. He also goes on, 'He will stand and shepherd his flock in the strength of the LORD...' (5:4a) taking on the role reserved for the LORD himself (Isa. 40:11). This is the true miracle of Christmas – the human shepherd would also be eternal God.

- X -

Who laid the earth with stone and rock
And cast the moon and stars in space?
Who balanced height and depth on earth,
The tides and waves that roll and chase?

Your Shepherd, Bethlehem; the clan
That will reveal the Son of Man.

We all like sheep have gone astray,
We all to weakness surrender,
But he will bring us to his way,
Our God, strong, gentle, and tender.

Part 3

Preparing for Christmas

PREPARING THE WAY

11th December

READ: Luke 1:5-25

'And he will go on before the Lord, in the spirit and power of Elijah, to turn the hearts of the parents to their children and the disobedient to the wisdom of the righteous—to make ready a people prepared for the Lord.'

Luke 1:17

C. S. Lewis once wrote about what he called the 'ages' of human life. First, there is the 'enchanted age' – the age of childlike wonder. Then we enter into the 'disenchanted age' – the age of cynicism. Finally, we make it to the 're-enchanted age' – the age of renewed wonder.[3] This is particularly evident when you think about Christmas. Growing up you are definitely in the enchanted age when it comes to Christmas. Everything is so exciting, joyous, and magical. However, when you get a bit older and some of the magic has gone you enter into the cynical disenchanted age, losing much of the wonder in the face of the realities and struggles of life. However, when you reach the stage of having children, grandchildren, or nieces and nephews, Christmas takes on a renewed wonder and you once again feel re-enchanted by the season of joy. Things are not as they were when you were growing up but they are no less exciting now that you see Christmas through the eyes of another. As a child you prepared your own heart for the joy of Christmas. Now you prepare for the joy of another and in so doing you receive a different kind of joy yourself.

John the Baptist's whole purpose in life was to prepare the way for someone else. Though he would be filled with the Holy Spirit from the womb (Luke 1:15), cause a stir through his preaching (3:3-18), and gain disciples (7:18), John understood that his calling was to point people to another. His life's task had been set before he was born. An angel announced to his father Zechariah, 'he will go on before the Lord, in the spirit and power of Elijah, to turn the hearts of the parents to their children and the disobedient to the wisdom of the righteous—to make ready a people prepared for the Lord' (1:17). How easy it could have been for John to let his popularity go to his head. Like his ancestors, he could have fallen into the temptation to 'do what was right in his own eyes.' Instead, he kept his eyes focused on the task God had given him and on the Saviour he had been called to announce. When the people speculated that he was the Messiah he replied, 'I baptise you with water. But one more powerful than I will come, the thongs of whose sandals I am not worthy to untie.' (3:16). Rather than seeing his calling as secondary, John considered it a joy (John 3:29) and willingly proclaimed, 'He must become greater, I must become less' (3:30). It takes humility to prepare for another and to put them first. But what greater joy can we have at Christmas than to prepare for the Saviour and declare with John, 'Behold, the Lamb of God, who takes away the sin of the world!' (John 1:29).

- XI -

What is a life not used for You
But rather filled with vain pursuit?
Spirit, prompt what I should do,
Disturb me 'til Your will takes root.

Announce the One so long foretold
Within the oracles of old.

Brothers, sisters, parents- see
God's power poured upon the earth!
A great drink offering he shall be,
Come treasure him for his great worth.

Make me lesser, put him first,
The One who cancels sin's great curse.

AN ADOPTIVE DAD

12th December

READ: Matthew 1:18-25

'But after he had considered this, an angel of the Lord appeared to him in a dream and said, "Joseph son of David, do not be afraid to take Mary home as your wife, because what is conceived in her is from the Holy Spirit.'

Matthew 1:20

I was a child of the 1980s. As I'm sure has become obvious, I love films and one of the most familiar faces of the movies of my childhood was a man called Rick Moranis. He starred in such films as: 'Ghostbusters', 'Little Shop of Horrors', 'Spaceballs', 'Honey, I Shrunk the Kids', and 'Parenthood'. However, by the late 90s he seemed to have completely disappeared. After seeing a re-run of one of the above films I decided to investigate what had happened to this beloved actor. I discovered that in the early 90s Moranis' wife had passed away and he became a single parent to his two children. In an interview he stated that if he continued to act, the amount of travel and time away from home would mean he couldn't be the type of dad he wanted to be to his children. He was a popular and successful actor but he was also a parent and he saw the latter role as much more important. Though he wouldn't have chosen to be put in the position of having to decide between his acting career and his children, it was never a question as to what was the priority. When asked if he regretted the decision Moranis said, 'I have absolutely no regrets whatsoever. My life is wonderful.'[4]

I can't even begin to imagine the emotions Joseph must have felt that first Christmas. There he was, a skilled carpenter engaged to be married to a beautiful young woman. The plans had likely already been set in place for the wedding and guests invited. Then in an instant his whole world is turned upside down. His bride-to-be tells him that she is pregnant, and he's not the father. Now, most men in that situation wouldn't have reacted well. Anger, confusion, and deep hurt would be the normal order of the day. However, Joseph's reaction to Mary is quite extraordinary. We read, 'Because Joseph her husband was a righteous man *and did not want to expose her to public disgrace*, he had in mind to divorce her quietly' (Matt. 1:19). Joseph didn't want to expose Mary to public disgrace. That's the complete opposite reaction to what we'd expect from most men today. But that's exactly why he would be the perfect adoptive dad for Jesus. The eternal Son had known the perfect love of the eternal Father, but he would also come to know the righteous, gentle, and yet imperfect love of the man who would take on the role as his earthly father. Of course, the angel informed Joseph of the truth, 'Joseph son of David, do not be afraid to take Mary home as your wife, because what is conceived in her is from the Holy Spirit. She will give birth to a son, and you are to give him the name Jesus, because he will save his people from their sins' (1:20-21). What a privilege; what a responsibility.

- XII -

For many years my hands have formed
A simple world with file and wood,
What son is this, not mine, yet ours;
Should our betrothal still conclude?

Good man, this son is from on high,
God's promised Day is drawing nigh.

The son is he who bids us come,
The Father's love to enter in;
Redemption through the Son of God
Makes sons and daughters of the King.

Resolved, I take him as my own,
My Saviour come as flesh and bone.

LEAPING FOR JOY

13th December

READ: Luke 1:39-45

'As soon as the sound of your greeting reached my ears, the baby in my womb leaped for joy.'

Luke 1:44

What gives you the most joy at Christmas? Maybe it's decorating the tree and covering your house with lights. It could be watching someone open the present you bought them and seeing the smile as they truly appreciate the gift you thought long and hard about before buying. Maybe it's the thought of the turkey and creamed potatoes; the Christmas pudding or the beautiful trifle (this is making me hungry). Or it might be the simple things like spending time with the ones you love. In light of recent world events, I think we've all come to appreciate the joy of spending time with other people. In our family it has been a long tradition (started before I was born) for the whole extended family (cousins, nieces, nephews and others) to meet together, share a meal, and exchange gifts on Christmas Eve. The food is consistently exceptional and the gifts are always well chosen, but the best part is just being with others that you love. Stepping out of the car and heading into my aunt's house I always get a rush of excitement. There's such a sense of joy when you meet again with someone you might not have seen since the previous Christmas Eve. Just being with them is something special.

Do you get the same rush of excitement and joy at the presence of Jesus? A man we thought about a couple of days ago certainly did; even before either of them was born! Just after the announcement of Jesus' birth, Mary sets off to visit her relative Elizabeth who is also pregnant with John the Baptist. When Mary arrives at her home the most incredible reaction ensues: 'When Elizabeth heard Mary's greeting, the baby leaped in her womb, and Elizabeth was filled with the Holy Spirit' (Luke 1:41). Don't you find that incredible? Here is a baby, as yet unborn, leaping with joy in his mother's womb because, by God's Spirit, he senses the presence of his Lord, who is also as yet unborn. Luke's choice of words are telling. The word translated 'leaped' here is used once more in Luke's gospel, by Jesus himself, in Luke 6:23 to describe how those who will partake in the blessing of the age to come will leap with joy. Also, the word translated 'joy' here expresses more than a mere feeling of happiness but is akin to 'exceedingly great joy' or 'exultation' that is most often used of those who are saved. John's recognition of Jesus went beyond anything we see in the other characters in the gospels. He has a pure joy in Jesus that comes only from a childlike faith produced by the power of the Holy Spirit. John was experiencing a joy in Jesus that is characteristic only of those who will enjoy the presence of God in the age to come. Is this your experience of the presence of Jesus?

- XIII -

Come over hill to see your kin
With laughter, tell each other's news,
Yet something else prompts deep within
The line well traced throughout the Jews.

The Spirit reaches through the womb
And leaps the babe! Could Christ come soon?

Here among us in our day?
Could eyes like ours be chosen to
Look upon the One who may,
No, will, see God's redemption through?

Blessed are you of woman born
To bring to pass Salvation's morn.

A MOTHER'S SONG

14th December

READ: Luke 1:46-56

'He has filled the hungry with good things but has sent the rich away empty.'

Luke 1:53

I vividly remember the moment I picked up my daughter for the very first time in the hospital. I held her like she was a piece of fine china and was overcome with a flood of emotions. I was filled with love for this little bundle and had an overwhelming feeling that I needed to keep her safe. However, none of these emotions were expressed on my face. One of the nurses told me that I looked terrified and in all honesty I probably was. Unlike my wife, my experience of caring for babies was very limited. I had briefly looked after our nephew one evening, but that was with the knowledge that he'd be returning home the next day. A large part of my terrified reaction was due to the fact that we now had responsibility for this little life. She would depend on us in the days and years ahead, not only for the basic necessities of life but also to show her the right way to live. She would inevitably look to us for guidance and copy us as she learned how to live and act. That meant that we had to be far more careful in what we said and did and be mindful that there was always someone there to mimic our behaviour. Without God's grace and leading the responsibility would have been too much for us. We always had to keep in mind that it was God who placed her in our care and at least he knew what he was doing!

As daunting as the prospect of raising our daughter might have been, think about the awesome responsibility entrusted to Mary and Joseph. The angel Gabriel had appeared to Mary and told her, 'You will be with child and give birth to a son, and you are to give him the name Jesus. He will be great and will be called the Son of the Most High. The Lord God will give him the throne of his father David, and he will reign over the house of Jacob for ever; his kingdom will never end' (Luke 1:31-33). Just imagine being given that level of responsibility – raising the Son of the Most High who will also be the fulfilment of all the promises we've been looking at throughout these reflections. The angel's words echo the great promise given to King David (2 Sam.7:13) and also Isaiah's incredible prophecy (Isa. 9:6). How does Mary react to this extraordinary news? 'I am the Lord's servant. May it be to me as you have said' (Luke 1:38). She expresses her feelings in the song of Luke 1:46-55. What comes across powerfully in this well-known song is the confidence Mary has in God and the delight she feels that the plans of the Lord are coming to pass in the child she will bear. She knows the birth of her child will mean justice for the oppressed (v. 53) and mercy for God's people (vs. 54-55). She focuses not on her own story but on God's story; the Christmas story. Mary teaches us what is most important. Maybe this year we need to focus our hearts and minds on God's story rather than our own.

- XIV -

Magnify the Lord, my soul,
Rejoice in him my Saviour!
For all the earth stands to be blessed,
In him I have found favour.

Before my time and after, he,
To those who fear him, shows mercy.

Brought low the mighty from their throne,
Raised up the lower together;
Abraham's seed comes forth in me-
Israel, your God remembers!

Before the Lord I bow my head,
May it so be as you have said.

TWO KINDS OF PEACE

15th December

READ: Luke 2:1-7

'In those days Caesar Augustus issued a decree that a census should be taken of the entire Roman world.'

Luke 2:1

It has become a modern stereotype across the world that when a contestant in a beauty pageant is asked what they desire the most, they will inevitably answer 'world peace.' To many the answer seems humorous and cliqued but in reality it is an ideal that most of humanity would aspire to. Hardly anyone today, with the exception of a few arms dealers, wants wars and conflicts to continue and most people would love to see 'peace on earth,' (a phrase most popular at Christmas time). Of course, many of us may assume that in our highly enlightened and developed modern societies we are getting closer and closer to that ideal. But the truth is, as John F. Kennedy pointed out, 'the mere absence of war is not peace.'[5] That's because we are involved in conflicts of many other kinds - in our relationships, in ethnic and racial tensions and even within ourselves. So what are we supposed to do? If we look to the world for answers, those answers will only ever address the symptoms of our problem. What we need is a peace that is comprehensive, one that gets to the heart of the problem.

Luke 2 begins, 'In those days Caesar Augustus issued a decree that a census should be taken of the entire Roman world' (2:1). For the modern reader, the mention of Caesar Augustus causes little reaction. We might just think, 'that's the bloke who gets a mention every Christmas.' However, for the first century reader, Augustus loomed large over the pages of history. He was the adopted son of Julius Caesar and the first Roman emperor. Augustus was not his name but a title that was bestowed on him which meant 'Majestic one'. As the son of the deified Caesar, he became known as 'the son of god.' He was hailed by his subjects as 'the saviour of the world.' His birthday was celebrated as the 'gospel' of the new beginning of the world and time itself was supposed to be marked by his birth. He took for himself the title '*Pontifex Maximus*' which means 'Greatest or Highest Priest'. He inaugurated the '*Pax Romana*' or the 'Roman Peace' and was seen by many to be the bringer of 'peace on earth.' So Caesar Augustus was seen as 'son of god', 'saviour of the world', 'the great high priest' and bringer of 'peace on earth' whose birth announced the gospel of a new world. Sound like anyone in particular? Luke seems to be contrasting two bringer of peace in the opening verses of this chapter – one who wielded immense power and the other born in humble surroundings. Augustus' peace came at the point of a sword. Jesus' peace came through his self-sacrificing love. Augustus' peace was short lived. The peace that Jesus brought will last forever. Which will you embrace this Christmas – the peace offered by the world or by the resurrected Saviour?

- XV -

What name is born of earthly lips
And seeks to rise above the rest?
What power, majesty or strength
Is claimed by man, but yet not blessed?

This babe is named by God on high,
For him this star moves in the sky

And shows where royalty is found;
The purest blood of human born,
High priest and Saviour in their full,
The gospel light of earth's new morn.

Augustus, bow the knee to him
Who comes to save the world from sin.

Part 4

Christmas Come

THE WORD BECAME FLESH

16th December

READ: John 1:1-14

'The Word became flesh and made his dwelling among us. We have seen his glory, the glory of the one and only Son, who came from the Father, full of grace and truth.'

John 1:14

I had the privilege of studying at a university in a small town called Aberystwyth, situated on the Ceredigion coast of Wales. It was surrounded by beautiful rolling hills and you were always in easy access of many a charming sandy beach. There were also plenty of ancient sites to keep the budding historian satisfied; from the Pendinas hillfort to the ruins of Aberystwyth Castle. But the most appealing thing about this seaside town was the almost nightly red and pink sunsets that hovered over the crashing sea. They were truly stunning and spectacular. The only problem was that after several months it became far too easy to take them for granted and not to notice this incredible display of God's artistry. What should have always elicited awe and wonder had just become a regular part of the surroundings. A few days ago I was reminded of the amazing beauty of those Welsh skies when I set off on one of my earlier morning runs and was presented with a similar sight. It made me erupt in praise to God and caused me to realise what I should have appreciated far more all those years ago.

Every Christmas we read these mind-blowing words at our carol services – 'The Word became flesh and made his dwelling among us.' I wonder, do you ever stop anymore to consider the magnitude of these words or do they wash over you like Bing Crosby telling you again that he's dreaming of a white Christmas? The Word, the second person of the Trinity, the agent of creation and the everlasting Lord became flesh – took on our humanity – and made his dwelling among us. This truth is spectacular on at least two fronts. First, in these words we see the beginning of the fulfilment of God's promise in the Garden to send a redeemer who would crush the head of the serpent. He would be a second Adam, completing what the first Adam failed to do and ushering in all the blessing that he forfeited through his rebellion. But this second Adam would be no ordinary man; God would do what he knew we could never do for ourselves by being born in human likeness and dying the humble death of a servant (Philippians 2:6-11). Second, by taking on our likeness he would also conform us to his likeness, making us heirs with him in glory (Rom. 8:29). As the great Church Father Athanasius put it, 'Christ became what we are that he might make us what he is.' Maybe you need to pause for a moment and mediate on this great truth – the eternal Word became flesh, made his dwelling among us, bore the guilt of our sins and gave us 'the right to become children of God' (John 1:12).

- XVI -

Slows spins the world this silent night,
Beneath the heavens opened up
To send their Maker to his earth,
To bear the cross and drink the cup.

Oh breathe, tired Earth, for starts the day
That loosens bonds to your decay.

What word could ever fully tell
The wonder of the Promise kept,
Our second Adam, strong but frail,
As into our lost world he steps.

Christ; God, in human form, has come
So that in him we are brought home.

Come, Saviour, quick, and condescend
To rescue us from our poor state.
Pitch your tent among us here,
Do not desert us to our fate.

MAKING GOD KNOWN

17th December

READ: John 1:15-34

'No-one has ever seen God, but God the One and Only, who is at the Father's side, has made him known.'

John 1:18

What is the scariest thing you've been asked to do? Quite a number of years ago while living and working in England, my wife and I had been asked by a friend of her family if we wanted to make a bit of extra money helping out at a dinner party she was hosting. This person was well-known in that community and attracted some prominent guests including a few celebrities. I thought that all we would be doing was serving some drinks and nibbles to the guests. What I wasn't expecting was to be asked to act as a valet, parking the guests' cars in the large field beside the house. At one point a classic Jaguar pulled up at the front of the house and out stepped the actor and comedian Chris Barrie (of 'Red Dwarf' and 'Brittas Empire' fame). He handed me the keys to the Jaguar and asked me to park it for him but to be very careful. To say that I was nervous would be a massive understatement. Not only was the car worth more than my house but it also belonged to a well-known celebrity. It was one of the scariest moments in my life. Thankfully I managed to park it without any real issues. What I never told anyone at the time was that I had only passed my driving test a few months before!

As we have mentioned before in these reflections, God had given Israel an awesome task – he had called them to make him known to the world around them; to declare his glory among the nations (Psalm 67; 96:3). Not only was this a great privilege, it was an awesome responsibility and no easy task. Most of the surrounding nations worshipped multiple gods while Israel worshipped one God. The gods of the nations were visible, made by human hands with gold, silver and wood. The God of Israel was invisible, and as the apostle Paul would later say, '...is not served by human hands, as if he needed anything. Rather, he himself gives everyone life and breath and everything else' (Acts 17:25). Israel was to be a light to the nations. But as we know, they failed in this calling. Instead, God promised that he would send another Servant Israel to complete the task (Isa. 49:6). This Servant was uniquely placed to make God known because he himself was, as John tells us, 'God the One and Only, who is at the Father's side...' (John 1:18). This brings us right back to the beginning and to Jesus' prayer in John 17. The Son had come to reveal the glory of God to humanity and now he calls us to make him known to the world. We are to declare the praises of the one who called us out of darkness and into his glorious light (1 Peter 2:0). It might seem like a scary task but it's also a great privilege. What better time than Christmas to make his name known?

- XVII -

Reveal the Light, the One true God
Of Jacob, Abraham and more,
Against the idols made of wood,
Of stone, and gold, and polished ore.

Israel, your task has failed
But my great Servant will prevail.

The Word of God who speaks out life
Will come to you, a Servant low
Sent from the Father's side; his life
Reveals the One from long ago.

He made our God's great glory known
And bids you go spread his renown.

He reveals the Father's face,
His love for fallen humankind,
Who ransoms, heals, restores the lost,
And gives true sight back to the blind.

PEACE ON EARTH, PEACE IN HEAVEN

18th December

READ: Luke 2:8-14

'Glory to God in the highest, and on earth peace among those with whom he is pleased!'

Luke 2:14

'Give my head peace!' This has to be one of the most popular sayings among folk from Northern Ireland and it has entered into the consciousness of the wider culture through a local comedy show of the same name. It's our way of saying 'stop bothering me' and indicates that the only way to get any peace is to be left alone. It seems that in daily life our concept of 'peace' never really extends beyond the desire to have a bit of space to relax in the busyness of the day. Ironically, Christmas (the season of peace) seems to be the one time of the year when we experience little of this peace. However, the Bible's concept of peace is something quite different. The Hebrew word '*Shalom*' means something more akin to 'wholeness', 'completeness', or 'fullness' in which every aspect of life works in perfect harmony. It covers every dimension of life – from family life and work to religious life and leisure pursuits. It's this kind of peace that we all need, yet it's not the kind of peace most of us are pursuing. As long as we get a rest in the midst of our hectic lives we seem happy to settle for less. As C. S. Lewis wrote, '…we are far too easily pleased.'[6]

A few days ago we looked at two kinds of peace; the peace offered by the world and the peace offered by the Messiah. The peace we were primarily thinking about at that time was peace with one another. It was this type of peace that the angels announced to the Shepherds at the birth of Christ: 'Glory to God in the highest, and on earth peace among those with whom he is pleased!' (Luke 2:14). But Jesus was bringing humanity more than peace with one another; he was also bringing us peace with God. Interestingly, similar words to those declared by the angels were proclaimed at the other end of Jesus' life as he rode into Jerusalem on Palm Sunday. The crowd that was hailing him as Messiah cried out, 'Blessed is the king who comes in the name of the Lord! *Peace in heaven and glory in the highest*!' (Luke 19:38). In both cases the phrase 'glory in the highest' and 'peace' are closely associated. However, at Jesus' birth it is peace among humans and at the triumphal entry it's peace in heaven. It's vitally important for us to understand that Jesus didn't just come to deal with the enmity among humans but also the enmity between God and humanity. The Bible makes clear that because of our sin we were all at one time enemies of God (Rom. 5:10) but now we have peace with God through our Lord Jesus Christ (Rom. 5:1). The peace that Jesus gives is comprehensive and it is this peace that we celebrate, sing about, and proclaim at Christmas.

- XVIII -

Shepherds cower at the sight
Of glory shining in the sky,
The Angels sing across the night
With praises to the God Most High:

Good news! Great joy! For see the day,
The Saviour lies among the hay.

All praise to God for his great grace,
His light meets darkness, overwhelms,
Sing high and low for peace on earth
Extends to peace in heaven's realms.

For heaven bridged the great divide,
Sufficient grace has been supplied.

Peace, O peace, the weary soul
Can rest in You and be restored.
The path is opened up to heaven
And we are enemies no more.

THE ORIGINAL SCROOGE

19th December

READ: Matthew 2:1-8, 16-18

'*When King Herod heard this he was disturbed, and all Jerusalem with him.*'

Matthew 2:3

Christmas just wouldn't feel like Christmas without Charles Dickens' classic 'A Christmas Carol'. It's one of the bestselling stories of all time and has been adapted on multiple occasions for theatre, radio, TV, and film. The central character, Ebenezer Scrooge is literature's ultimate crusty, fun-hating, tight-fisted villain. Scrooge cares little about the needs and desires of those around him and seeks only to look after number one. It's only after the ghosts of Christmas past, present, and future show him the consequences of his behaviour that his life is miraculously changed and he starts to seek the betterment of others. His self-centred life was one marked by misery and gloom. His transformed life was one marked by joy and true happiness. Though Dickens had a peculiar view of the Christian faith, Scrooge illustrated for him the true marks of the converted man – one who looked not only to his own interests but also to the interest of others (Philippians 2:4).

Long before Dickens wrote his Christmas classic there was a man associated with Christmas who made Scrooge look like an angel. That man was the Judean king Herod.

Herod was of Edomite descent and therefore had no rightful claim to the throne in Judea. He was given the title 'king of the Jews' by Octavian (Caesar Augustus) and he governed as a Roman ally for around 33 years. Because of this, Herod was mostly despised by the Jews. He tried hard to win the favour of the people by building them a lavish temple but even this didn't work. He was tolerated by most and loved by few. Herod was well aware of the expectation among the Jewish people of the time that a coming Messiah would take up his throne in Jerusalem. Herod feared that such a person would cause him to lose his position and power. That's what we see in the account given in Matthew 2. Magi from the east arrive in Jerusalem asking the question that Herod feared the most: 'Where is the one who has been born king of the Jews? We saw his star in the east and have come to worship him' (2:2). Matthew tells us the reaction of Herod and his court: 'When King Herod heard this he was disturbed, and all Jerusalem with him' (2:3). He immediately calls for the chief priests and teachers of the law to ask them where Scripture says the Messiah is to be born. They read to him from Micah 5 that he would be born in Bethlehem. After failing to get the Magi to tell him the specific location he sends to have all the male children from two years old and under killed (2:16). But his plan failed. Unlike Scrooge, there was no redemption for Herod. The child he tried to kill would take his throne and Herod would become another obscure figure from history. God's long-promised plan could not be thwarted by the original Scrooge.

- XIX -

The royal ears prick fear, and twitch
His eyes to see these foreign men
Ask where the King is to be found
So they can go to worship him.

The Magi told, 'do all you can'
To bring about your evil plan.

Your fear of losing power grows,
They will not say where he is laid,
Your core brings forth your malice, fear,
With little lives your dread is paid.

This child whose life you aim to take,
A true King of the Jews will make.

He reigns all time, you turn to dust,
He rose again while you decay
Into the earth his hands have made;
He formed you from the dirt and clay.

CHRISTMAS WORSHIP

20th December

READ: Matthew 2:7-12

'On coming to the house, they saw the child with his mother Mary, and they bowed down and worshiped him. Then they opened their treasures and presented him with gifts of gold, frankincense and myrrh.'

Matthew 2:11

It's customary every Christmas for Christians to complain about the 'commercialization' of Christmas. We hear things like, 'We've completely lost the real meaning of Christmas' or 'They're just trying to take Christ out of Christmas.' The ironic thing is that those of us who do the most complaining secretly love a well-decorated tree, the exchange of gifts, and several days of eating too much food. I wonder if we were asked to put our money where our mouth is, would we be willing to let go of all these things? The answer is: probably not. At a push, I'd be willing to give them all up but what I just couldn't give up is the singing of carols, the reading of the Christmas lessons and hearing the message of Christ's incarnation. Christmas without worship just isn't possible. That means that what most people in the Western world call 'Christmas' is something else altogether. If it excludes the worship of the Lord it has no right to the name.

Matthew 2 contains one of the very first Christmas worship services. Magi from the east (traditionally Persia) travel many miles to attend this worship service. They had been following a star which they believed would lead them to a great king. 'Wise men' as they were (though the text never tells us this) they go to the place where you're most likely to encounter a new king – the palace in Jerusalem. There they meet a king unworthy of the name who can't hide his jealousy at the thought that a rival king might be in the vicinity. The Magi make clear that they have come with a very specific purpose: '...we saw his star when it rose and have come to worship him' (2:2). King Herod makes a pretence of wanting to do the same (2:8). But these men weren't simply going through the motions like so many people at carol services all over the world. They had travelled for many miles over many days to worship this new-born king. As we read in verse 11, 'On coming to the house, they saw the child with his mother Mary, and they bowed down and worshiped him' (2:11a). The gifts that they brought for this new-born king indicates the value they placed on him (2:11b). Gold, incense, and myrrh are not inexpensive items. I wonder if the same intense longing to worship Jesus is in our hearts as well. Do we pretend like Herod, go through the motions like so many in the world today, or are we willing to go to great lengths to lay down our treasures before the king and worship him? Like the Magi, may it be this Christmas that the most important thing we do is worship the one who is Saviour, Lord, and King!

- XX -

Go through the door, this humble place
That hides Messiah come at last.
Accept the off'ring given to
The promised One of ages past.

No gift could ever take the place
Of Christ the child sent down in grace.

To feel the worth of Christ in full,
If possible within our frame,
Confines all else to lesser place
And puts at top his precious name.

Forbid that we would lose the weight
Of why we celebrate this date.

Remove from us those lesser things
That draw our eyes and heart from his
Great mercy, grace and majesty.
Show us who our treasure is.

Part 5

The Message of Christmas

TELLING THE STORY

21st December

READ: Luke 2:15-18

'When they had seen him, they spread the word concerning what had been told them about this child, and all who heard it were amazed at what the shepherds said to them.'

Luke 2:17-18

Can you remember the excitement of Christmas morning when you were a child? Running down stairs (unless you lived in a bungalow) and flinging open the living room door to behold the presents that Santa (don't judge me) had left under the tree. I have two older brothers and one of the very first things I wanted to do on Christmas morning – even before playing with my toys – was to tell both of them what gifts I had received. The experience never seemed complete without sharing it and telling others about it. I was so overwhelmed with joy that it was probably extremely difficult to understand a word I was saying as it all came out in a jumbled garble of excitement. I didn't want to keep the joy to myself and couldn't wait to tell all my friends about my presents and to find out about theirs. If something is worth experiencing then it is also worth sharing.

I'm pretty certain that when the shepherds left the baby in the manger and went to tell others what they had seen and heard it probably came out as a bit of a garbled mess of excitement. Think about what they had experienced. They had seen the awesome and terrifying sight of an angel surrounded by the shining glory of the Lord declaring to them, 'Do not be afraid. I bring you good news of great joy that will be for all the people. Today in the town of David a Saviour has been born to you; he is Christ the Lord' (Luke 2:10). These humble shepherds had been given the news the people of God had been waiting to hear for centuries. The Messiah from David's line had arrived and he would be the Saviour and Lord of his people. However, these unexpected recipients of this good news were told that they would find the Messiah in the most unexpected of places: 'You will find a baby wrapped in cloths and lying in a manger' (2:12). If all of this wasn't strange enough they were then confronted by a heavenly choir of angels singing about the glory of God and peace on earth (2:14). They eventually found the child in the manger with Mary and Joseph and we are told, 'When they had seen him, they spread the word concerning what had been told them about this child…' (2:17). The shepherds just couldn't keep it to themselves, they had to tell others this amazing news. Luke records the reaction to it: '…and all who heard it were amazed at what the shepherds said to them' (2:18). Have you ever considered that the message the shepherds felt compelled to share with others is the same message we have the privilege of sharing every Christmas. Let's share that news with the same excitement of a child on Christmas morning.

- XXI -

"Let us go over to Bethlehem
For there is much that we must surely see"
So left the Shepherds with haste to stir them,
To go forth, find the child, and bend the knee.
They came to Mary and Joseph and child,
Watched over while he in a manger lay,
This trough from which animals rough and wild
Would feed, a bed for this King in the hay.
But the Shepherds were sure they had seen him,
The One whom the angels in song proclaimed,
So rise, spread news of the babe and the hymn,
Declare how this child by the Lord had been named.
Once really seen, the Christ in his glory,
All within us wants to share the story.

PONDER THESE THINGS
22nd December

READ: Luke 2:16-20

'But Mary treasured up all these things and pondered them in her heart.'

Luke 2:19

'Familiarity breeds contempt.' This old saying reminds us that when we become overly used to something we lose some of the joy in it and might even begin to resent it. We have become so familiar with the Christmas stories that they might just pass over us with little effect, even if we haven't yet come to the extreme of resenting them. Part of the problem is that we don't give these stories the type of attention they really deserve. Many of us get so busy with other things that we find little time to give our full attention to the stories that have given us the Christmas season in the first place. But think about doing this in any other sphere of life. If you brushed off your friends with a five minute meet up once a year, would you consider that a healthy relationship? If you're married, imagine taking your spouse out for an extremely rare meal only to gobble down the food as fast as you can, ask for the bill before they are finished, just so you can get home to watch the telly. Yet this is exactly what many of us do with the Christmas stories. We read parts of the stories as one-liners in Christmas cards, hear them read in a carol service while our eyes glaze over thinking about the other duties of the day or dash through them in our quiet times (if we have them in the first place). Is that the kind of respect these stories warrant?

Luke includes a detail in his account of the Christmas story that shows us that at least one person gave these events the kind of attention they deserved. After the shepherds depart from visiting the baby we are told: 'But Mary treasured up all these things and pondered them in her heart' (Luke 2:19). She 'treasured up' and 'pondered' them. The word translated 'treasured up' means to keep something in mind so that it will not be forgotten and the word translated 'pondered' speaks of mediating upon and bringing all the events together in the mind until they become embedded in the heart. Of course, we might say that Mary was a witness to the events in question and was a participant in them so it's little wonder that she recorded them away in her heart. Also, this was the birth of her first son and what mother can forget a day like that! But what were 'all these things' that verse 19 speaks of that Mary treasured up and pondered? Well, it wasn't just the birth of her son but also the message conveyed to her by the shepherds which had been proclaimed by the angels. That message was about who her son was – 'a Saviour…he is Christ the Lord' (2:10). Mary was mediating upon the Christmas story itself and the fulfilment of all the promises God had made to his people right from the beginning. This was a story that deserved time, attention, and appropriate consideration. As those who possess the rest of the story, we ought to be those who ponder these things in our hearts!

- XXII -

The Shepherds leave the family in joy,
The words of proclamation ringing still
About their precious child, this infant boy,
The Lamb who will God's great Promise fulfil.
The Son and Saviour, precious little one
Looks up at her now in both love and need.
She savours every moment with her son,
The gift humanity has now received.
Oh my heart and soul do not soon forget
These great things that are stored within my chest.
In time when he is fully grown please let
Them comfort me when I would be distressed.
A shadow looms over this child of mine,
I know that I shall be bereft in time.

FROM THE CRADLE TO THE CROSS

23rd December

READ: John 19:25-27

'When Jesus saw his mother there, and the disciple whom he loved standing nearby, he said to her, "Woman, here is your son," and to the disciple, "Here is your mother." From that time on, this disciple took her into his home.'

John 19:26-27

Sometimes it's a blessing not to know the future. I don't know if you're anything like me but when I've been watching something on TV recently that was made a few years ago I keep thinking, 'you have no idea what's going to happen in the future.' I wonder if it would have changed the way we lived if we had known beforehand about the pandemic. We might not have been able to stop it but we certainly would have had a stronger appreciation for the things that we probably took for granted. Would we have treasured those times with family and friends more if we knew that our contact with them was going to be limited? When I think about the future for our daughter and her generation it can sometimes be depressing to consider the challenges they are likely to face. Although I hope and pray that the generation to come will stand firm in the Lord, I'm glad that I don't know the future. That's not for you or me to know, we are called to live faithfully one day at a time.

Yesterday we left Mary treasuring up and pondering in her heart all the wonderful things she had heard and experienced at the birth of Jesus. Had Mary known every detail of what her son was going to have to face some 30 years later, she might well have despaired. When taking the baby Jesus to be circumcised she was made aware of something tragic that would happen to him in the future. At the temple one of the priests, Simeon, held Jesus in his arms and declared to Mary, 'Behold, this child is appointed for the fall and rising of many in Israel, and for a sign that is opposed (and a sword will pierce through your own soul also)' (Luke 2:34-35). What Mary couldn't have known was that Jesus' appointed path would be from the cradle to the cross. Years later when she stood below the cross, shedding tears at the pain, abuse, and ridicule suffered by her son, she must have felt totally helpless. Every time Jesus fell and cut his knee as a child while playing with his brothers and sisters, Mary would have been there to comfort her boy. But here she was, powerless to intervene. She couldn't hold him; she couldn't whisper to him that everything was going to be okay. It's astounding that in this moment of great despair, as Mary longs to comfort Jesus, he comforts her from the cross. John records the powerful and poignant moment when Jesus calls the apostle to take care of Mary as his own mother (John 19:26-27). Jesus always knew that the cradle would lead to the cross; Christmas would lead to Easter. There, tragedy would turn to triumph; death to everlasting life.

- XXIII -

How then this? God's Promise is surely lost,
My son beaten a black and royal blue,
His hands and feet nailed to a cruel, crass, cross;
His striped human flesh ripped and pierced straight through.
Is this the great plan foretold for my son?
Her baby, now grown, looks down on her grief,
He will dry her tears, when raised he has won,
And sin and death is no more that great thief.
Take this woman who has loved me so well
From that time when Shepherds and Magi came,
This pain of yours is no lasting death knell;
Through me life bursts out over sin and shame.
Dear woman, this was always meant to be;
From crib to cross, Salvation's plan was me.

THE PURPOSE OF THE STORY

24th December

READ: Luke 24:13-27

'He said to them, "How foolish you are, and how slow to believe all that the prophets have spoken! Did not the Messiah have to suffer these things and then enter his glory?" And beginning with Moses and all the Prophets, he explained to them what was said in all the Scriptures concerning himself.'

Luke 24:25-27

When most people look at a nativity scene what do you think is going through their minds? If it's in a shop they're most likely thinking, 'That would make a great decoration.' Others will simply see it as a quaint representation of an ancient myth, akin to any other fairy tale. What do you see? What I see when I look at a nativity scene is a small part of a much larger story. Over the past few weeks we have tried to consider the bigger story into which the nativity (and all the passages associated with Christmas) fit in. To stay at the 'stable' is to reduce the story to a soundbite and to miss that Jesus is the central character in a cosmic drama that is leading to the transformation of this world. The Christmas story will just become another clichéd part of the holiday season, like any number of other elements that come to mind at this time of year, unless we reclaim the story that makes Christmas so truly remarkable.

The story God's people had lived through was both wonderful and tragic. It was marked with many highs and not a few lows. Abraham was promised the blessing of a people, a place, and God's presence; the things forfeited by Adam. But first the people had to endure centuries of slavery. Moses and Joshua brought the people to the place God had promised but they almost forfeited God's presence because of their sin. God raised up a great king to rule over them, yet David's descendants were both righteous and rogues (the rogues being more numerous). The kingdom was divided and the people exiled from their place. The temple was destroyed and God's presence departed. The temple was rebuilt but the glory did not return as it had before. That was until a man from Nazareth walked into the temple proclaiming himself to be the great 'I AM' (John 8:58). This man declared himself to be the bread of life, water for the thirsty, the light of the world, the shepherd of God's people, the only way to the Father, and the true vine that Israel had failed to be. In other words, this man – born to David's line – was announcing that Israel's story, humanity's story, found it's fulfilment in him. He had come to purchase a people, bring them to a paradise place and manifest to them the presence of God in a way they had never experienced. Yet the people missed the point. That's why after his resurrection he showed them the purpose of the story they had always been told. He was the purpose; he was the point – 'And beginning with Moses and all the Prophets, he explained to them what was said in all the Scriptures concerning himself" (Luke 24:27).

- XXIV -

Come search the pages of the Holy book
With me and see me there in every page,
I am the scarlet thread if you would look,
The one long expected from age to age.
From Adam's foul Fall when God did first pledge
That Eve's own Descendant would yet bring forth
Healing, redemption that removed the wedge
Between God and man; O praise his great worth!
Israel, your story is now fulfilled
In Christ, the Messiah, who ends our strife,
And who offers himself to all who will
Accept him as Lord and King of their life.
From the start to the end it has been me;
My life, death, and rising now makes you free.

THE SECOND ADVENT

25th December

READ: Colossians 3:1-4

'When Christ, who is your life, appears, then you also will appear with him in glory.'

Colossians 3:4

If you're reading this on Christmas Day I want to wish you a Merry Christmas. I don't know what you'll be doing today but I hope to enjoy good food, good chat, and maybe even a couple of good carols. One of my favourite carols, and one of the most popular, has to be 'Joy to the World.' But what's funny is that it's not really about the Christmas story at all but about Christ's Second Coming – it's not about the First Advent but about the Second Advent. Isaac Watts had written the hymn as a Christian paraphrase of Psalm 98. Psalm 98 is a glorious vision of what is yet to come as the world rejoices at its restoration. That Watts was thinking about the Second Coming can be seen particularly in the lyrics, 'No more let sins and sorrows grow, nor thorns infest the ground; He comes to make His blessings flow far as the curse is found'. Here is the undoing of Adam's curse and the proclamation of a new heaven and new earth won by Christ (see, Isa. 65:17-19; 2 Peter 3:10-13; Rev. 21:1-4). And yet, the hymn is not altogether inappropriate for this time of year because what Christ began to do at his first coming he will complete at his second coming; they are two parts of the one story.[7]

Christians live at a strange time in history. We are described as strangers and exiles in this world (1 Peter 2:11) as well as citizens of heaven who await a Saviour from there (Philippians 3:20). The author of Hebrews compares us to the people of Israel wandering through the wilderness as they journeyed toward the Promised Land and their promised rest. You could say that we live between two Christmases. We live in that period between Christ's First's Advent, when he came as suffering servant to die for the sin of his people, and the Second Advent, when he will finally make all things new; completely restoring his people and creation, and ruling as conquering king. So how ought we to live in this inter-advent period? The apostle Paul wrote to the Colossians, 'Since, then, you have been raised with Christ, set your hearts on things above, where Christ is seated at the right hand of God. Set your minds on things above, not on earthly things. For you died, and your life is now hidden with Christ in God. When Christ who is your life, appears, then you will appear with him in glory' (Col. 3:1-4). We are to set our hearts and minds on things above, not on earthly things. Christmas is one of those times when it's very difficult not to be distracted by earthly things. That's why we need to be reminded again and again that our true life is hidden with Christ in God. Who we truly are is not yet seen but when Christ returns all will behold the glory he came to reveal to the world. May God bless you this Christmas.

- XXV-

Come exiles, strangers, citizens
And join the feast of Christ the Lord;
Brothers, sisters, in the babe
Who came to die, yet rose, adored
By those he came to free from death
And sin, and loss, and every dark
Deception, promising new life
For those who trust in his great work.

Celebrate the babe once born
To waken sweet redemption's morn.

Gather saints; in sin yet new,
Peel bells across the frozen earth,
Feast with joy this happy day
And sing out songs that praise his worth.
Near and far across the globe
God's chosen people join with voice
Those hidden in the Saviour's love;
Sons and daughters, come rejoice!

Christ shall come again in strength,
Not poor in manger but in might,
And bring to close his saving work
That started with this silent night.

Endnotes

1 This phrase is slightly adapted from the work of Graeme Goldsworthy. See, Graeme Goldsworthy, *The Goldsworthy Trilogy* (Milton Keynes: Paternoster, 2008) 54.

2 Jean M. Twenge and W. Keith Campbell, *The Narcissism Epi demic: Living in the Age of Entitlement* (New York: Atria, 2009) 48.

3 Adapted from, C. S. Lewis, 'Talking About Bicycles' in Walter Hooper (ed.), *Present Concerns* (London: Fount, 1986) 67-72.

4 https://www.hollywoodreporter.com/movies/movie-features/rick-moranis-reveals-why-he-829779/

5 President John F. Kennedy, 1963 State of the Union Address, January 14, 1963.

6 C. S. Lewis, *The Weight of Glory and Other Addresses* (New York: HarperCollins, 2001) 26.

7 For more details see, the Gospel Coalition article 'Joy to the World: A Christmas Hymn Reconsidered' by Alyssa Poblete - https://www.thegospelcoalition.org/article/joy-to-the-world-a-classic-christmas-hymn-reconsidered/

* 9 7 8 1 6 4 9 6 0 1 9 3 3 *
BV - #0045 - 211021 - C0 - 215/143/5 - PB - 9781649601933 - Gloss Lamination